The Porcelain God Speaks:
Deep Thoughts From The Bathroom Wall
© 2005 by Jacque Lynn Schiller

Published by Ig Publishing
178 Clinton Avenue
Brooklyn, NY 11205
www.igpub.com
igpublishing@earthlink.net

ISBN: 0-9703125-4-7

10 9 8 7 6 5 4 3 2 1

The Porcelain God Speaks

(Deep thoughts from the bathroom wall)

Jacque Lynn Schiller

designed by
Charles Orr

Acknowledgement should be paid to family and friends whose contributions made this project possible, and special recognition afforded to all the anonymous authors compelled to brandish a marker or take lipstick to the walls of history.

I FEEL SO STRONGLY
ABOUT TOILET GRAFFITI,
I SIGNED A PARTITION.

Introduction

In an age where daily affirmations are gleaned via advertising taglines, the proverbial 15 minutes of fame is bestowed upon the marginally talented and handwritten sentiments have been left by the wayside in deference to email, a universal source providing human connection must be found. Humanitys voice at contemplative rest may provide just such instruction, within the confines of lifes laboratory, the lavatory. Due to its inherent privacy, the loo offers the newly born poet the chance to leave his/her mark, to connect with an unknown friend, or to vent an unseemly frustration. All that is needed is a wall, a stall, and a pen to place the world on notice.

The following pages represent my humble attempt to categorize the lessons and illustrate the camaraderie so wondrously prevalent in latrinalia, with the hope that from such humble beginnings true wealth might be shared by all.

Words of Wisdom

Tired of greeting card platitudes and computer generated thoughts-of-the-day, modern philosophers have adopted a more egalitarian approach to dispensing information. Body in repose, mind at ease, one is open to unimaginable possibilities.

CHEAP ART IS GOOD FERYA.

Maps

that lie

flat lie

Until your face melts, it's all great.

Guest Check

SERVER	TABLE	GUESTS	CHECK NUMBER
			872679

At the
feast
of ego,
everyone
leaves
hungry.

	TAX	
Thank You	TOTAL	

a adams 210

The reason is simple.

NEVER TRUST
A SMILING DOG

HISTORY IS NOT SO IMPORTANT.

It's all
fun and games
until somebody
gets eaten.

SUPPORT BACTERIA,
IT'S THE ONLY CULTURE
MOST PEOPLE HAVE

Nostalgia

isn't what it

used to be.

The **MAIN** thing is
to keep the thing
the thing.

One man's laughter is

-.. . ..-. .. -. .
(Define)

-.-- --- ..- .-.
(your)

... -.-- -- -... --- .-.. ... .-.-.-
(symbols.)

nother manslaughter.

You can want

what you will,

but you cannot

will what you want.

I am, therefore I think
(at least I think I am)

Lost Literature

Unjust as book burning, and paralleling Pompeii's swift demolition, the prose-filled walls of some wayside diner or nightclub loo can be rendered silent with a perfunctory swipe of paint. Fortunately, the flames of momentary inspiration cannot be forever extinguished.

**Where talent,
there lies.**

delirious and obsessive play. A delirious

delirious and obsessive play. A delirious and obsessive play. A delirious and obsessive play. A de

Milk the cow

Feed the hen

My life is yours

You kill.

A delirious and obsessive play. A delirious and obsessive play. A delirious and obsessive play. A delirious and obsessive play. A delirious and obses

Someday When.

Life is Words.

Drink is the curse of the working man.

Work is the curse of the drinking man.

Drink is the work of the cursing man.

The Devil drives a Buick

and eats his lunch inside;

He sticks his pitchfork

through the trunk

and pulls out the spare tire –

true love.

Let's party for the apocalypse when
she will come out of the dirt like a little flower.

Ambiguity is
the Devil's
Tether-ball.

When God made man he made him out of string, he had a little left so he left a little thing.

When God made woman he made her out of lace, he didn't have enough so he left a little space.

Sometimes
I wish I was
What I was
when
I wished I was
What I am now.

All alone in a world meant for others
Ye who stand forsaken by God
You howl but nobody bothers
They smile & distantly nod
For its true inside you're not like them
Not happy with playing your role
And though you wish the truth would spike them
You hide from them heart and soul.
Who could you ask when they lack understanding
Who could you tell that you're not of their kind
Could your belief be
True is there a wolf in you
what could they
find inside your mind.
Lycanthropy is not just an insane delusion
It's real, in spirit, heart & body

**Evil has many tools
and a lie is a handle
that fits them all.**

I hope this makes it to you my
wolf-sister, my friend
For you must know that like hearts can one another mend.
You are not so alone, so alone as you feel.
I understand this wolf pain
And the anguish is real
I hold it too
Buried deep in my soul
and it burns into me
light blue flaming coal
But I fear not and find
Hope in the few, who
understand the hurt
people like you.

I am on the verge of insanity

knocking on the door of truth.

The door opens and I find

I've been knocking from the inside.

Location Location Location

Would the works of Michelangelo be less glorious if housed some place other than the Sistine Chapel? When environment and content work in tandem the viewer is riveted by its cleverness.

For a copy of
these walls,
write 'Walls'
Pueblo, CO 81005

This is where the dicks hang out.

Play Toilet Tennis...

Look Left on the right wall...

You've got
the whole world
in your hands

If you can piss this high, join the fire department.

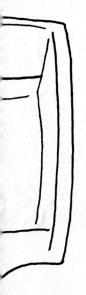

Look Right

Shakespeare
before leaving.

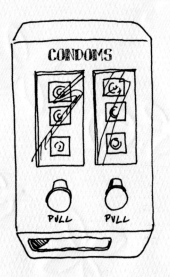

As much pleasure as your boyfriend, with the added bonus of usefulness!

Ancient Forest Dispenser

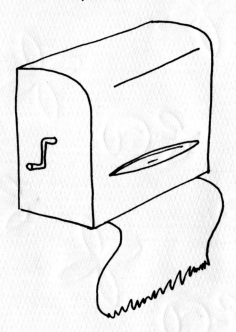

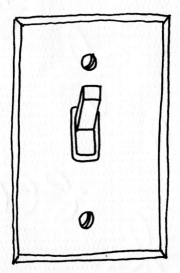

Don't touch.
Dart thrower.

Think!...

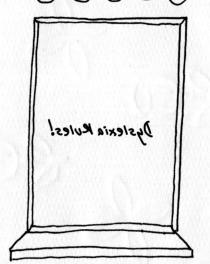

...Thoap!

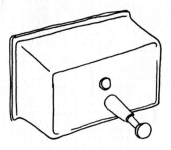

Free Cowboy Hats

FOR SEAT COVER-
PULL UP
THEN PULL DOWN

Women

Women have long gathered to commiserate, gossip or to simply lend a shoulder to cry on. Therefore it should come as no surprise to find this support system extended to the W.C., where a steady stream of consciousness is most welcome and equally lauded.

Cinderella is drunk

and has lost her shoe.

There's no broken heart that a margarita

and open toed shoes can't mend.

If you disagree with someone,

you should always walk a mile in her shoes.

Then, if you still disagree, she'll be barefoot and

you'll have a one mile lead.

Woman's faults are many,

Men have only two

Everything they say

and everything they do.

The check i$ in the male.

The best way to a man's heart is to saw his breast plate open.

If I were a beauty queen,
would I be in this position?

What do the toilet seat

and a g-spot have in common?

Men miss them every time.

If you wipe more than once
you're playing with yourself.

Some of the ladies of the court

liked to curl up with a good book,

but most preferred a page.

A Woman's Rule of Thumb:

If it has tires or testicles,

you're going to have trouble with it.

Support woman's lib –

make him sleep in the wet patch

I hate periods.

Well, you might want to try one of the English language's many other forms of punctuation. May I suggest a comma?

You're too good for him.

Save trees. Eat more beaver.

I caught a 20 lb. salmon once.
I wanted to mount it,
but there were people there.

Q: Why is a bungee cord

the same as a prostitute?

A: They both cost 50 bucks

and if the rubber breaks you die.

8-80. Blind, crippled or crazy I'll do em all!

be a hero and crap on the ceiling.

No matter how
good she looks,
some other guy
is sick and tired
of putting up
with her shit.

Any loser can piss on the floor,

Woman

is a sperm depository

which gets malfunctional

once a month.

Remember -

more than three shakes

is a wank.

When life hands you a lemon,

pull out a gun and start shooting.

I screwed your mother!

Go home Dad, you're drunk.

Do not throw toothpicks

Beauty is only a light switch away.

I want to get screwed.

Buy a Ford.

into urinal, Crabs polevault.

Love, Hate,
and Marking One's Territory

Talk shows and self-help book sales would have one believe that communication within relations is vital in order to sustain a happy life together. However, a trip to the local port-a-potty betrays this economic-driven fallacy. The battle of the sexes rages on.

Could I tell you I miss you?

Nobody's perfect...

until you fall in love with them.

Stung by cupids direct bow loves

My wife follows me everywher

I DO NOT.

go astray he shall

arrow buried quick but shall he ever

lose his prick..

Christine.

If you're

reading this,

we're through.

I pretend love you too.

Nobody's perfect...

until you fall in love with them.

Necrophilia means never
having to say I'm sorry.

You can't put a bag

over personality.

Out of Left Field

Though I can not say for certain, it is my strong opinion that the fast pace of daily existence has produced a peculiar yet nonetheless entertaining phenomena noted as a blip but colloquially referred to as the "brain fart."

Breast milk gives you eyelashes.

Unpleasantly

A pickle is not a pickle unless _____.

oose flow

Babies are delicious.

Leather sponges.

Aside from that,

Mrs. Kennedy,

how was the parade?

I only hear pleasant sounds.

Always believe there is something.

My   fell off today.

arm

Non-non ___ is the least evil.

Ezekiel with

the shaved head

used to be

Elijah with the

shaved legs.

Don't forget to bring my celery.

But until then we should fill the world with happy little trees

I have the strength

of a bear who has

the strength of two bears!

Religion

While religion is said to be a taboo subject for the dinner table, it appears open for discussion a few hours afterward.

JESUS SAVES! ...AND GRETZKY SCORES!

God knows why you're doing this, but...

God isn't watching you always.

Jesus Saves Souls!
...and turns them in for
Fabulous
Cash
Prizes!

Jesus is coming soon!

Quick! Look busy!

Does your vision of Jesus

look like Barry Gibb

from the Bee Gees?

Jesus

♥ **U**

...The rest of us think
you're an asshole

...but only as a friend

Jesus Christ is coming soon!

... to a theatre near you!

JESUS $AVES

...but wouldn't it be better if he had inve$ted?

But God did layeth

a smacketh

down on the Egyptians.

Going to church doesn't make you

a good person any more

than standing in a garage

makes you a car.

Jesus saves!

...and so can you at Wal-mart.

Voice of the People
Protest Takes to the Stalls

Freedom of speech is an inalienable right too often discouraged. But in this booth one can cast a different kind of vote, sling a distinctive brand of mud without fear of retribution. With the punctuation of a toilet's flush, "Let Freedom Ring!"

The Hippies Will Rise Again.

But The Day Will Be Half Over.

If voting

could really change things,

it would be illegal.

Bread not Bombs

We tried bread

and found it would not explode.

If you voted for Clinton in the last election, you can't take a dump here. Your asshole is in Washington.

Stop Imperialism Against Madonna.

Marx didn't know
that Bismarck would invent
unemployment insurance.

**JOIN THE ARMY,
MEET INTERESTING
PEOPLE AND KILL THEM.**

Don't change Dicks
in the middle of a screw,
Stick with Nixon in '72!

Nixon did for America
what pantyhose did for fingering.

If pro is opposite of con,

then what is

the opposite of progress?

Congress!

Bushes are for pissing on.

Frodo has failed,
Bush has the ring

DRUNKEN FRAT BOY DRIVES
COUNTRY INTO DITCH.

It's time to trim the Bush.

Hans Blix -- look over here.

Free Soviet Jews

...inside specially marked packages of

Kellogg's Rice Krispies!

Daddy, can I start the war now?

Fighting for peace

is like screwing for virginity.

WHO WOULD JESUS BOMB?

WWJD

I asked for

universal health care

and all I got

was this lousy

stealth bomber.

An eye for an eye

leaves the whole world blind.

- Gandhi

Lightbulb Moment

Many an "a-ha!" moment has been expelled while expelling.

You mean this is not a storage space?

IT'S MY PARENTS FAULT MORE THAN THE DRUGS

raise

I've decided that to   my grades
I must   my standards.

lower

It's hard to make a comeback
when you haven't been anywhere.

I should really learn to read.

We should eat
people instead.

6 6 8

is the neighbor of the Beast!

Life's like a pubic hair on toilet seat -

you soon get pissed off.

The lemmings were

p
u
s
h
e
d
!

Rehab is for quitters.

Only users lose drugs.

Tolkien is hobbit forming.

I have a PBS mind in an MTV world.

Little Red Riding Hood

is a small Russian contraceptive!

Life is like a shit sandwich.

The more bread you have,

the less shit you have to eat.

Is There Anybody Out There?

There comes a time in everyone's life when they feel alone, that no one is listening. Possibly the symbolism of drains present in the pissoir propels one to leave their mark, proof of existence in a solitary act. Hopefully this was true when these were written.

I make a living

scraping coke

off the floor.   A bathroom

without a mirror,

oh now really!

Gordon, surface for air.

Fight for the rights of the pansexual!

Does that mean you screw a
little guy with hooves and a flute?

and what role if any
is played by the flute?

It plays an octave, albeit minor, role.

If you need vocals to rock, you suck!

If only you'd use
your powers for good
instead of evil...

Is sado-masochistic
necrophiliac bestiality
flogging a dead horse?

My mother made me a whore.

If I give her the yarn,
will she make me one too?

I Love Grils!

It's Spelled Girls.

WHAT ABOUT
US GRILS?

Will trade
one blind crab
for one
without teeth.

I'm pink, therefore I'm SPAM.

Id give my right arm

to be ambidextrous.

Eschew obfuscation.

Insanity is to art what garlic is to salad.

Waiter, there's too
much garlic in my salad.

I vandalize because
I realize vandalism
is humanism.

I once was blind;
Now I'm just lost.

Everybody

Go Homo Sapiens!

I AM NOT YOUR TARGET MARKET!

Not all who wander are lost.

Not all who launder are washed.

What's worse, Ignorance or Apathy?

I don't know and I don't care!

Shut

What if the hokey pokey IS what it's all about?

Life is one
contradiction
after another.

No it's not!

I firmly believe
the sounds of
Ratt and Motley Crue
will be back.

Up!

Zen

It seems only appropriate to close this book with a koan of sorts, a final offering to meditate on. A word is a mere symbol of the true object it represents. A picture within a picture, a rose is a rose is a rose...even when surrounded by manure.